DEFEATING YOUR
RECKLESS
DRIVING
TICKET IN VIRGINIA

by **Attorney Michael C. Huff**

Jacobs & Whitehall
73-03 Bell Blvd, #10
Oakland Gardens, NY 11364
www.jacobsandwhitehall.com

Ordering Information:

Quantity sales. Special discounts are available on quantity purchases by corporations, associations, and others. For details, contact the publisher at the address above.

Orders by U.S. trade bookstores and wholesalers. Please contact Jacobs & Whitehall: Tel: (888) 991-2766 or visit www.jacobsandwhitehall.com.

Printed in the United States of America

Published in 2020

ISBN: 978-1-951149-49-9

DISCLAIMER

This publication is intended to be used for educational purposes only. No legal advice is being given and no attorney-client relationship is intended to be created by reading this material. The author assumes no liability for any errors or omissions, for how this book or its contents are used or interpreted, or for any consequences resulting directly or indirectly from the use of this book. For legal or any other advice, please consult with an experienced attorney who is aware of the specific facts of your case and is knowledgeable of the judges in your jurisdiction.

Huff Law, PLC
11815 Fountain Way, Suite 300
Newport News, Virginia 23606, USA
(757) 394-3434
www.hufflawplc.com

TESTIMONIALS

"This is the second time that I have hired Mr. Huff as my attorney and with both cases I have been 100% satisfied with his results. When I first called and had our consultation he laid everything out right in front of me. Unlike other lawyers he didn't start out with his payments but instead addressed my case and gave me multiple avenues of approach. He is very approachable and comfortable to talk to in person or over the phone. When it comes time for court he is exceptionally presentable, clever and is willing to play "hard ball" if you so choose. When it comes to lawyers you usually get what you pay for. He is very reasonably priced but I couldn't help but feel I got more than my monies worth. I have already referred him to two people and will continue to do so."

— Cade

****

"I live/work out of state and was hesitant to choose a lawyer I could not meet in person. Attorney Michael Huff went above and beyond for my case. After I failed to obtain some of the documents his office requested as evidence for my case, and after I was delayed responding to all of his correspondence, he was still readily available to answer all my questions and present my case in court. Most significantly, even without the documents, he was able to get my charges reduced. Highly recommend to anyone, especially those in need out of state."

— Molly

****

4

"I was involved in a road rage incident and the other driver accused me of assault and battery and reckless driving. Mr. Huff walked in with so much confidence and owned the courtroom. He knew the exact questions to ask and he KNOWS the law! Someone I knew referred him to me and I am 100% satisfied with him as an attorney for any case I may need assistance with. Excellent job Attorney Huff!"

– Nichelle

****

"This was the first time I had gotten a traffic ticket (Reckless Driving). Mr. Huff was referred to me by a coworker since I'm new in the area. He was very helpful from the beginning when I called him for a consultation. We got a great verdict, will definitely refer him in the future."

– Jennifer

****

I got a "failure to yield" ticket for a traffic accident I was involved in. A friend had just gotten his Reckless Driving ticket taken care of with Michael and gave me his card. I called and Michael was able to get the case dismissed!

– Jenna

****

TABLE OF CONTENTS

ABOUT THE AUTHOR

My name is Michael C. Huff and I am a criminal defense attorney in Virginia. I received my Bachelor's degree in Political Science from Christopher Newport University and my Juris Doctor degree from Washington and Lee University School of Law. I am licensed to practice law in the Commonwealth of Virginia.

I handle all types of criminal cases ranging from minor traffic tickets to life-sentence felonies. Compared to any other type of misdemeanor or felony, the most common crime I see is Reckless Driving, which is not only a traffic ticket, but is also a class 1 misdemeanor. I have literally handled thousands of these cases. Because of that, I have decided to write this book. This book is specifically focused on the criminal offense of Reckless Driving in Virginia.

Why Did You Write This Book?

I wanted to write this book because Reckless Driving cases are very common and most people do not understand the seriousness of the charge. People need to be educated on the severity of a Reckless Driving ticket and what can be done to avoid a criminal conviction. This book is for anyone charged with a Reckless Driving ticket in Virginia.

People from all walks of life get charged with Reckless Driving. However, a lot of people are unaware that a Reckless Driving ticket is essentially a traffic ticket on steroids. It is not a minor traffic infraction. It is actually a criminal offense - a class 1 misdemeanor in fact. That is the most severe type of misdemeanor. A conviction of a class 1 misdemeanor carries with it a permanent criminal record, a potential jail sentence of a maximum of 12 months, and a potential fine of a maximum of $2,500. That puts the crime of Reckless Driving in the same boat as the crimes of Assault and Battery, Larceny, DUI, or Intentional Destruction of Property, etc., all of which are also class 1 misdemeanors.

In addition, a conviction of Reckless Driving carries with it a potential suspension of your driver's license for a maximum of 6 months, demerit points on your driving record, and increased car insurance rates. If you have a commercial driver's license ("CDL"), it could be impacted or revoked due to a conviction of Reckless Driving. This could, in turn, cause you to lose your job or prevent you from obtaining a job that requires a CDL.

Even if you are not a resident of Virginia, the criminal conviction would still follow you on your criminal record. And, as of the date of this book, there is no provision under Virginia law that will allow you to hide, expunge, seal, or have that criminal conviction removed from your criminal record.

Consequently, if an employer were to utilize a federal government system to conduct a criminal background check on you, it would show that you have been convicted of a class 1 misdemeanor for Reckless Driving. You would have to disclose that conviction on job applications, various license applications, and security clearance applications if the application asks if you have ever been convicted of a misdemeanor.

I have also written this book because I do not want people to be misled or scared by online blogs and attorneys that use scare tactics to lure people into hiring them. Since there is a variance in information about these charges online and in the real world, it can be misleading and confusing for anyone. You cannot always trust what you read online, even if it is from an attorney because you do not know anything about that attorney. Is that attorney licensed to practice law in Virginia? Does that attorney work in the particular court in which you are charged? Does that attorney know your particular judge? Does that attorney handle these types of cases? Does that attorney know what he or she is doing? Does that attorney know all of the technical defenses to a Reckless Driving ticket? There are a lot of unknowns. Therefore, I have decided to write this book as a means to provide completely accurate and precise information about Reckless Driving tickets as opposed to what people may read online or hear from another attorney.

CHAPTER 1

WHAT IS RECKLESS DRIVING IN VIRGINIA?

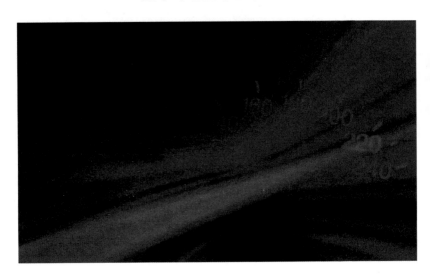

There are 15 types of Reckless Driving tickets in Virginia. I will list the three most common types of Reckless Driving tickets first and then the remainder in numerical order of their code section.

1. Reckless Driving By Speed

Reckless Driving By Speed is punished under Virginia Code §46.2-862. That law states:

Va Code §46.2-862. Exceeding speed limit.

A person is guilty of reckless driving who drives a motor vehicle on the highways in the Commonwealth (i) at a speed of 20 miles per hour or more in excess of the applicable maximum speed limit or (ii) in excess of 85 miles per hour regardless of the applicable maximum speed limit.

Under this law, there are two ways that you can be convicted of Reckless Driving By Speed. The police officer must be able to prove that you drove either 20 mph or more over the posted speed limit or 86 mph or higher regardless of the posted speed limit.

For example, it is considered Reckless Driving By Speed if you drive 75 mph in a posted 55 mph zone or 86 mph in a posted 70 mph zone.

This is basically a speeding ticket on steroids. This is the most common type of Reckless Driving offense hands down. A police officer can determine your speed with a radar gun, laser gun, or the pace method. A radar gun has a range of up to about 5,000 feet, which is about a mile away from the police officer. A radar gun can be used when the police officer is either parked or driving in any direction relative to you. A laser gun has a range of up to about 2,000 feet, which is about a 1/3 mile away from the police officer. A laser gun can be used only when the police officer is parked, not while he or she is driving. Furthermore, unlike a radar gun, a laser gun should not be used when it is located behind the police officer's glass windshield or on a day with any type of precipitation. The "pace method" requires the police officer to follow behind your car at a constant speed and at an equal distance for at least 2/10 of a mile. Once this is done, the police officer will look at the speedometer in his or her police car to determine your speed. The pace method is valid only when the police officer first catches up to your vehicle and then begins the pace method. The pace method is not valid if the police officer begins the pace method while he or she is still in the process of trying to catch up to your vehicle. Regardless of the method used to determine your alleged speed, Virginia law requires that the police officer bring to court the calibration paperwork that proves his or her radar gun, laser gun, or police car's speedometer has been tested for its accuracy within 6 months before the date you received your ticket.

Notably, there is a similar, non-criminal charge in Virginia called "Speeding 20 mph+," which punishes you for driving 20 mph or more over the posted speed limit.

However, that charge is seldomly used by police officers as they typically elect to charge a driver with Reckless Driving By Speed instead.

2. Reckless Driving Generally

Reckless Driving Generally is punished under Virginia Code §46.2-852. That law states:

Va Code §46.2-852. Reckless driving; general rule.

Irrespective of the maximum speeds permitted by law, any person who drives a vehicle on any highway recklessly or at a speed or in a manner so as to endanger the life, limb, or property of any person shall be guilty of reckless driving.

Under this law, the police officer must be able to prove that you drove in a manner that endangered the life, limb, or property of any person, including yourself. This can be proven by your speed, erratic or crazy driving, distracted driving, impaired driving, impatient driving, or risk-taking driving. There is no specific driving behavior that you need to display in order to be convicted of this offense. Instead, it could be any driving behavior that the judge or jury considers as reckless driving. This law is the "catch-all" version of Reckless Driving. There is no requirement that you get into an accident in order to be convicted of this offense.

For example, it is considered Reckless Driving Generally if you accelerate too quickly, drive too fast for the road or weather conditions at the time, tailgate other cars, constantly change lanes, weave in-and-out of traffic, straddle multiple lanes, drive on the shoulder of the road, drive on the opposite side of the road, fall asleep behind the wheel, or are distracted to a point where your driving behavior fails.

Notably, if you were charged with this offense after getting into an accident, there is case law that holds that the mere happening of an accident does not automatically equal reckless driving.

3. **Reckless Driving Failure To Maintain Control/Improper Brakes**

Reckless Driving Failure To Maintain Control/Improper Brakes is punished under Virginia Code §46.2-853. That law states:

Va Code §46.2-853. Driving vehicle which is not under control; faulty brakes.

A person shall be guilty of reckless driving who drives a vehicle which is not under proper control or which has inadequate or improperly adjusted brakes on any highway in the Commonwealth.

Under this law, there are two ways that you can be convicted of Reckless Driving Failure To Maintain Control/Improper Brakes. The police officer must be able to prove that you either drove a vehicle that was not under proper control or drove a vehicle with inadequate or improperly adjusted brakes. There is no requirement that you get into an accident in order to be convicted of this offense.

For example, it is considered Reckless Driving Failure To Maintain Control/Improper Brakes if you accelerate too quickly or speed and lose control, drive too fast for the road or weather conditions at the time and lose control, tailgate other cars and lose control, constantly change lanes and lose control, make an erratic or unsafe lane change and lose control, weave in-and-out of traffic and lose control, fall asleep behind the wheel and lose control, are distracted to a point where you lose control, or drive a vehicle with inadequate or improperly adjusted brakes.

Notably, if you were charged with this offense due to getting into an accident on a snowy or rainy day, there is case law that holds that mere hydroplaning does not automatically equal reckless driving.

4. **Reckless Driving By Passing Another Vehicle On Top Of A Hill Or Curve**

Reckless Driving By Passing Another Vehicle On Top Of A Hill Or Curve is punished under Virginia Code §46.2-854. That law states:

> *Va Code §46.2-854. Passing on or at the crest of a grade or on a curve.*
>
> *A person shall be guilty of reckless driving who, while driving a vehicle, overtakes and passes another vehicle proceeding in the same direction, on or approaching the crest of a grade or on or approaching a curve in the highway, where the driver's view along the highway is obstructed, except where the overtaking vehicle is being operated on a highway having two or more designated lanes of roadway for each direction of travel or on a designated one-way roadway or highway.*

Under this law, the police officer must be able to prove that you — while driving on a two-way road with one lane going in each direction — passed another vehicle driving in the same direction as yourself while on or approaching the top of a hill or a curve and your view along the road was obstructed. This law punishes you for passing another vehicle by driving on the shoulder or in the oncoming traffic lane while having an obstructed view of the road ahead. This law does not apply to you if you are driving on a one-way road or a two-way road with two or more lanes going in each direction.

For example, it is considered Reckless Driving Passing Another Vehicle On Top Of A Hill Or Curve if you — while driving on a two-way road with one lane going in each direction — drive in the oncoming traffic lane in order to pass another vehicle driving in the same direction as yourself while approaching the top of a hill with an obstructed view of oncoming traffic.

5. **Reckless Driving By Driving With Obstructed View/Impaired Control**

Reckless Driving By Driving With Obstructed View/Impaired Control is punished under Virginia Code §46.2-855. That law states:

19

Va Code §46.2-855. Driving with driver's view obstructed or control impaired.

A person shall be guilty of reckless driving who drives a vehicle when it is so loaded, or when there are in the front seat such number of persons, as to obstruct the view of the driver to the front or sides of the vehicle or to interfere with the driver's control over the driving mechanism of the vehicle.

Under this law, there are two ways that you can be convicted of Reckless Driving By Driving With Obstructed View/Impaired Control. The police officer must be able to prove that you drove a vehicle that was loaded in the front seat with so much stuff or so many people that it either obstructed your front or side views outside the vehicle or interfered with your control over the driving mechanism of the vehicle.

For example, it is considered Reckless Driving By Driving With Obstructed View/Impaired Control if you drive with two passengers in your front passenger seat and those passengers block your view outside the front-passenger side window or their legs get in the way of your gear shifter.

6. Reckless Driving By Passing Two Vehicles Abreast

Reckless Driving By Passing Two Vehicles Abreast is punished under Virginia Code §46.2-856. That law states:

Va Code §46.2-856. Passing two vehicles abreast.

A person shall be guilty of reckless driving who passes or attempts to pass two other vehicles abreast, moving in the same direction, except on highways having separate roadways of three or more lanes for each direction of travel, or on designated one-way streets or highways. This section shall not apply, however, to a motor vehicle passing two other vehicles when one or both of such other vehicles is a bicycle, electric personal assistive mobility device, electric power-assisted bicycle, or moped; nor shall this section apply to a bicycle, electric personal assistive mobility device, electric power-assisted bicycle, or moped passing two other vehicles.

Under this law, the police officer must be able to prove that you — while driving on a two-way road with two lanes going in each direction — passed, or attempted to pass, two other vehicles that were side-by-side with each other and driving in the same direction as yourself. This law punishes you for passing two side-by-side vehicles by driving on the shoulder or in the oncoming traffic lane.

This law does not apply to you if you are driving on a one-way road or a two-way road with three or more lanes going in each direction. This law does not apply to you if you are passing a bicycle or moped, or are riding one yourself.

For example, it is considered Reckless Driving By Passing Two Vehicles Abreast if you — while driving on a two-way road with two lanes going in each direction — drive in the oncoming traffic lane in order to pass two side-by-side vehicles driving in the same direction as yourself.

7. Reckless Driving By Driving Two Vehicles Abreast In A Single Lane

Reckless Driving By Driving Two Vehicles Abreast In A Single Lane is punished under Virginia Code §46.2-857. That law states:

Va Code §46.2-857. Driving two abreast in a single lane.

A person shall be guilty of reckless driving who drives any motor vehicle so as to be abreast of another vehicle in a lane designed for one vehicle, or drives any motor vehicle so as to travel abreast of any other vehicle traveling in a lane designed for one vehicle. Nothing in this section shall be construed to prohibit two two-wheeled motorcycles from traveling abreast while traveling in a lane designated for one vehicle. In addition, this section shall not apply to (i) any validly authorized parade, motorcade, or motorcycle escort; (ii) a motor vehicle traveling in the same lane of traffic as a bicycle, electric personal assistive mobility device, electric power-assisted bicycle, or moped; nor shall it apply to (iii) any vehicle when lawfully overtaking and passing one or more vehicles traveling in the same direction in a separate lane.

Under this law, the police officer must be able to prove that you drove side-by-side with another vehicle in the same lane when that lane was designed for just one vehicle.

For example, it is considered Reckless Driving By Driving Two Vehicles Abreast In A Single Lane if you pass another vehicle without completely leaving your original lane.

8. Reckless Driving By Passing At A Railroad Crossing, Intersection, Or Pedestrian Crossing

Reckless Driving By Passing At A Railroad Crossing, Intersection, Or Pedestrian Crossing is punished under Virginia Code §46.2-858. That law states:

Va Code §46.2-858. Passing at a railroad grade crossing.

A person shall be guilty of reckless driving who overtakes or passes any other vehicle proceeding in the same direction at

any railroad grade crossing or at any intersection of highways
unless such vehicles are being operated on a highway having
two or more designated lanes of roadway for each direction of
travel or unless such intersection is designated and marked as
a passing zone or on a designated one-way street or highway,
or while pedestrians are passing or about to pass in front of
either of such vehicles unless permitted so to do by a traffic
light or law-enforcement officer.

Under this law, the police officer must be able to prove that you — while driving on a two-way road with one lane going in each direction — passed another vehicle driving in the same direction as yourself at a railroad crossing or roadway intersection; or that you passed another vehicle while pedestrians were passing or about to pass in front of your vehicle or the other vehicle. This law punishes you for passing another vehicle at a railroad crossing or roadway intersection by driving on the shoulder or in the oncoming traffic lane, and for endangering pedestrians. If you are passing at a railroad crossing or roadway intersection, this law does not apply to you if you are driving on a one-way road or a two-way road with two or more lanes going in each direction.

For example, it is considered Reckless Driving By Passing At A Railroad Crossing, Intersection, Or Pedestrian Crossing if you — while on a two-way road with one lane going in each direction — drive in the oncoming traffic lane in order to pass another vehicle driving in the same direction as yourself while at a railroad crossing.

9. Reckless Driving By Passing A Stopped School Bus

Reckless Driving By Passing A Stopped School Bus is punished under Virginia Code §46.2-859. That law states, in pertinent part:

> *Va Code §46.2-859. Passing a stopped school bus; prima facie evidence.*
>
> *A person driving a motor vehicle shall stop such vehicle when approaching, from any direction, any school bus which is stopped on any highway, private road or school driveway for the purpose of taking on or discharging children, the elderly, or mentally or physically handicapped persons, and shall remain stopped until all the persons are clear of the highway, private road or school driveway and the bus is put in motion; any person violating the foregoing is guilty of reckless driving. The driver of a vehicle, however, need not stop when approaching a school bus if the school bus is stopped on the other roadway of a divided highway,*

25

on an access road, or on a driveway when the other roadway, access road, or driveway is separated from the roadway on which he is driving by a physical barrier or an unpaved area. The driver of a vehicle also need not stop when approaching a school bus which is loading or discharging passengers from or onto property immediately adjacent to a school if the driver is directed by a law-enforcement officer or other duly authorized uniformed school crossing guard to pass the school bus.

Under this law, the police officer must be able to prove that you failed to stop or remain stopped for a stopped school bus that was equipped with warning signs and flashing lights at the time it was stopped to load or unload passengers, and that you were driving on a road without a physical barrier or an unpaved area separating you from the school bus. You must come to a complete stop even if the passengers have not yet begun to load or unload. You must remain stopped until all passengers are completely clear of the road and the bus starts moving again. This law does not apply to you if there is a physical barrier or an unpaved area, such as a grassy or concrete median, separating you from the school bus.

For example, it is considered Reckless Driving By Passing A Stopped School Bus if you drive past or fail to remain stopped at a stopped school bus that has its flashing lights on and its stop sign out to unload passengers and there is no median separating you from the school bus.

10. Reckless Driving By Failing To Signal

Reckless Driving By Failing To Signal is punished under Virginia Code §46.2-860. That law states:

Va Code §46.2-860. Failing to give proper signals.

A person shall be guilty of reckless driving who fails to give adequate and timely signals of intention to turn, partly turn, slow down, or stop, as required by Article 6 (§ 46.2-848 et seq.) of this chapter.

Under this law, the police officer must be able to prove that you failed to give an adequate and timely signal of your intention to turn, partly turn, slow down, or stop to another vehicle that was close enough to be affected by your movement. If you intend to turn, partly turn, slow down, or stop and there is another vehicle close enough to you to be affected by your movement, you must give the proper turn signal, light signal, or hand signal so that your intention to make such movement is plainly visible to the other vehicle. You must continuously signal your intention for at least 50 feet if the posted speed limit is 35 mph or less, or for at least 100 feet if the posted speed limit is 40 mph or higher.

For example, it is considered Reckless Driving By Failing To Signal if there is another vehicle 25 feet behind you in an adjacent lane and you change into that adjacent lane without using your turn signal.

11. Reckless Driving By Excessive Speed For The Road Conditions

Reckless Driving By Excessive Speed For The Road Conditions is punished under Virginia Code §46.2-861. That law states:

> *Va Code §46.2-861. Driving too fast for highway and traffic conditions.*
>
> *A person shall be guilty of reckless driving who exceeds a reasonable speed under the circumstances and traffic conditions existing at the time, regardless of any posted speed limit.*

Under this law, the police officer must be able to prove that you drove too fast for the road or weather conditions at the time. During traffic congestion or inclement weather, you are required to slow down and adjust to a safe speed given the road or weather conditions at the time. You must do this even if you have to drive slower than the posted speed limit. It is reckless driving if the speed you are driving is simply too risky or dangerous for the current road or weather conditions at the time. You do not need to exceed the posted speed limit in order to be convicted of this offense.

For example, it is considered Reckless Driving By Excessive Speed For The Road Conditions if you drive 68 mph in a posted 70 mph zone during a snowstorm or heavy rain.

12. Reckless Driving By Failure To Move Over Or Yield To An Emergency Vehicle

Reckless Driving By Failure To Move Over Or Yield To An Emergency Vehicle is punished under Virginia Code §46.2-861.1. That law states, in pertinent part:

Va Code §46.2-861.1. Drivers to yield right-of-way or reduce speed when approaching stationary vehicles displaying certain warning lights on highways; penalties.

A. The driver of any motor vehicle, upon approaching a stationary vehicle that is displaying a flashing, blinking, or alternating blue, red, or amber light or lights as provided in § 46.2-1022, 46.2-

1023, or 46.2-1024 or subsection B of § 46.2-1026 shall (i) on a highway having at least four lanes, at least two of which are intended for traffic proceeding as the approaching vehicle, proceed with caution and, if reasonable, with due regard for safety and traffic conditions, yield the right-of-way by making a lane change into a lane not adjacent to the stationary vehicle or (ii) if changing lanes would be unreasonable or unsafe, proceed with due caution and maintain a safe speed for highway conditions. A violation of any provision of this subsection is reckless driving.

Under this law, the police officer must be able to prove that you — upon approaching a parked emergency vehicle displaying flashing blue or red lights — failed to either move over into an adjacent lane away from the emergency vehicle or slow down to a safe speed while next to the emergency vehicle. This is the newest addition to the Reckless Driving catalog of charges. This is known as Virginia's "Move Over" law and it became a Reckless Driving offense in 2019.

For example, it is considered Reckless Driving By Failure To Move Over Or Yield To An Emergency Vehicle if you — upon approaching a parked police car with its flashing blue lights on — fail to move over into an adjacent lane away from the police car or slow down to a safe speed while next to the police car.

13. Reckless Driving By Failure To Stop/Yield To Right-Of-Way

Reckless Driving By Failure To Stop/Yield To Right-Of-Way is punished under Virginia Code §46.2-863. That law states:

Va Code §46.2-863. Failure to yield right-of-way.

A person shall be guilty of reckless driving who fails to bring his vehicle to a stop immediately before entering a highway from a side road when there is traffic approaching on such highway within 500 feet of such point of entrance, unless (i) a "Yield Right-of-Way" sign is posted or (ii) where such sign is posted, fails, upon entering such highway, to yield the right-of-way to the driver of a vehicle approaching on such highway from either direction.

Under this law, the police officer must be able to prove that you were driving on a side road and failed to stop or yield before entering a road with another vehicle on it approaching you within 500 feet. This law punishes you for cutting off another vehicle when entering from a side road. If you are entering from a side road and there is another vehicle on the road you intend to turn onto and that vehicle is within 500 feet of you, you must either stop or yield. If the side road does not have a stop or yield sign, you must come to a complete stop before entering that road. If the side road has a stop sign, you must come to a complete stop no matter what, even if no other vehicle is approaching you. If the side road has a yield sign, you must simply yield to the right-of-way before entering the road.

For example, it is considered Reckless Driving By Failure To Stop/Yield To Right-Of-Way if you are on a side road that does not have a stop or yield sign and you fail to stop when turning onto a road with another vehicle on it approaching you 250 feet away.

14. Reckless Driving In A Parking Lot

Reckless Driving In A Parking Lot is punished under Virginia Code §46.2-864. That law states:

Va Code §46.2-864. Reckless driving on parking lots, etc.

A person is guilty of reckless driving who operates any motor vehicle at a speed or in a manner so as to endanger the life, limb, or property of any person:

1. On any driveway or premises of a church, school, recreational facility, or business or governmental property open to the public; or

2. On the premises of any industrial establishment providing parking space for customers, patrons, or employees; or

3. On any highway under construction or not yet open to the public.

Under this law, the police officer must be able to prove that you — while either in a parking lot, on a private road, or on a public road under construction/not yet open to the public — drove in a manner that endangered the life, limb, or property of any person, including yourself. This can be proven by your speed, erratic or crazy driving, distracted driving, impaired driving, impatient driving, or risk-taking driving. There is no requirement that you get into an accident in order to be convicted of this offense. This offense is identical to Reckless Driving Generally under Virginia Code §46.2-852. The only difference is that this offense must occur either in a parking lot, on a private road, or on a public road under construction/not yet open to the public whereas the offense of Reckless Driving Generally must occur on a public road.

For example, it is considered Reckless Driving In A Parking Lot if you — while either in a parking lot, on a private road, or on a public road under construction/not yet open to the public — speed, accelerate too quickly, drive too fast for the road or weather conditions at the time, back out of a parking spot or reverse too quickly, drive over parking spots, tailgate other cars, fall asleep behind the wheel, or are distracted to a point where your driving behavior fails.

15. Reckless Driving Racing

Reckless Driving Racing is punished under Virginia Code §46.2-865. That law states:

Va Code §46.2-865. Racing; penalty.

Any person who engages in a race between two or more motor vehicles on the highways in the Commonwealth or on any driveway or premises of a church, school, recreational facility, or business property open to the public in the Commonwealth shall be guilty of reckless driving unless authorized by the owner of the property or his agent. When any person is convicted of reckless driving under this section, in addition to any other penalties provided by law the driver's license of such person shall be suspended by the court for a period of not less than six months nor more than two years. In case of conviction, the court

34

shall order the surrender of the license to the court where it shall be disposed of in accordance with the provisions of § 46.2-398.

Under this law, the police officer must be able to prove that you drove in tandem with another vehicle for the purpose of engaging in a race or competition. This law applies to you on a private and public road. You do not need to exceed the posted speed limit in order to be convicted of this offense.

For example, it is considered Reckless Driving Racing if you and another vehicle each accelerate rapidly for the purpose of engaging in a competition with each other.

Notably, a conviction of this offense carries an enhanced punishment that includes a "mandatory" suspension of your driver's license for a minimum of 6 months up to a maximum of 2 years, whereas most other Reckless Driving offenses carry a "discretionary" suspension of your driver's license for a maximum of 6 months.

CHAPTER 2

HOW COMMON ARE RECKLESS DRIVING TICKETS IN VIRGINIA?

Reckless Driving tickets in Virginia are extremely common. The truth is that most people, to a certain extent, will speed or commit a minor traffic violation at some point in their lives. The catch to Reckless Driving is that it can be committed by anyone from all walks of life. You do not need to be a bad person or a criminal to get a Reckless Driving ticket. It can happen to anyone.

The majority of people in America drive and many do not realize how tough Virginia's traffic laws are compared to other states. Virginia has some of the toughest laws in America. People are not aware that Reckless Driving is a criminal offense and that a conviction of it can affect their freedom, potential job prospects, driver's license, and car insurance premium.

What Happens When Someone Is Pulled Over For Reckless Driving?

When you are pulled over or stopped by the police for Reckless Driving, the encounter will usually last between 5 to 15 minutes.

Getting pulled over starts with the police officer activating his or her emergency equipment — which refers to the strobe lights on top of his or her police car — to pull you over. If you happen to already be stopped or pulled over, the police officer can keep you stopped and detained at that location. It does not matter what state you are licensed in or where you live; if you are driving in Virginia, you have to abide by Virginia law.

The police officer will walk to your driver or passenger side window and ask for your driver's license and registration, or rental car agreement. It is a common protocol for the police officer to shine his or her flashlight on you, your passengers, and inside your car — especially at night. This is a safety procedure that allows the police officer to see if anyone is trying to harm the police officer or is in possession of illegal contraband.

Once you give the police officer your driver's license and registration, or rental car agreement, he or she will typically tell you why you were pulled over or stopped and the specific speed or driving behavior you are accused of. If you have been accused of Reckless Driving By Speed, the police officer is not required to show you his or her radar gun reading or radar calibration paperwork on the side of the road. If you have been accused of any other type of Reckless Driving, the police officer is not required to tell you what any witnesses said to him or her on the side of the road. It is common for the police officer to ask you why you were driving at the speed or in the manner in which you have been accused. Do not answer those questions or volunteer any information to the police officer.

After the police officer finishes explaining to you the basis of your Reckless Driving ticket, the police officer will return back to his or her police car for the purpose of running your driving and criminal record, running a warrant check to determine if there are any active warrants for your arrest, and writing you a Reckless Driving ticket.

The police officer will then walk back to you and hand you a yellow paper that indicates what specifically you have been charged with and your court date and time. That yellow paper is your Reckless Driving "ticket," "summons," or "charge" (they all mean the same thing). Sometimes your ticket is on white paper.

Notably, when someone is pulled over or stopped for Reckless Driving in Virginia, they are usually not arrested and taken to jail when they receive their Reckless Driving ticket. Although a police officer can make an arrest when issuing a Reckless Driving ticket, they normally do not. Instead, the police usually issue you a ticket and let you drive away and carry on with your day. A police officer will arrest you, however, if you are being charged with a more serious charge in addition to your Reckless Driving ticket, such as a drug possession, DUI, or felony charge, or if you have an active warrant for your arrest, etc.

The police officer is then going to ask you to sign your ticket to indicate that you promise to appear in court. Signing your ticket does not mean that you are admitting guilt to the alleged offense. It simply means that you acknowledge your court date and time and promise to appear in court or hire an attorney to appear in court on your behalf.

If you do not sign your ticket, the police officer can arrest you, take you to jail on the basis that you are a "flight risk" since you refused to sign your ticket, and let the magistrate at the jail decide whether or not to grant you bail and release you. Most people sign. And in actuality, the ticket states that by signing it, it is not an admission of guilt.

When issuing you your Reckless Driving ticket, the police officer will tell you that you must appear in court and that you cannot prepay the ticket without appearing in court. This rule applies to you no matter where you live in the world and regardless of any inconvenience it may cause to you and others. For a regular speeding ticket or a minor traffic offense, you can simply prepay the ticket without appearing in court and you usually do not need an attorney. But once you are charged with Reckless Driving, it is a game changer. Since Reckless Driving is a criminal charge, the rules change. You have to physically appear in court just like you would for any other criminal charge such as Assault and Battery, Larceny, DUI, or Intentional Destruction of Property, etc.

However, because Reckless Driving is a traffic-related criminal charge, some courts will allow you to stay at home if you hire an attorney and if your case has no realistic likelihood of you receiving a jail sentence. To determine if your case has a realistic likelihood of you receiving a jail sentence, please refer to page 78.

If you fail to appear in court for your Reckless Driving ticket and you do not have an attorney appear in court on your behalf, the judge will either resolve your case and convict you of Reckless Driving in your absence or keep your case open and issue an arrest warrant against you, which is called a "capias." That arrest warrant will be valid in all 50 states in America and any police officer in any city or state can arrest you and put you in their jail based on that arrest warrant. The bottom line is that you have to appear in court for a Reckless Driving ticket unless the court in which you are charged allows an attorney to appear on your behalf, and that varies from jurisdiction to jurisdiction.

Lastly, after you sign your ticket and the police officer tells you that you are free to leave, you may safely drive away.

Should I Answer Any Questions By Law Enforcement On The Roadside?

It is always ideal to be polite and cooperative with the police officer. However, that does not necessarily mean you have to provide a statement, explanation, apology, excuse, or defense to the police officer. You can kindly tell the police officer that you "respectfully invoke your right and privilege against self-incrimination and do not wish to answer any questions or make any statements."

In fact, it is wise not to make any statements to the police officer. This is because the police officer will undoubtedly write down notes of everything you said, take those notes to court, and tell the judge everything you said. Then, the judge will take your statements into account as evidence and factor that evidence into the equation of whether or not you are guilty of Reckless Driving. For example, statements such as "I had to use the bathroom," "My passenger is sick," "I have an emergency at home," "I am on my way to a funeral," "I did not see that car because

I was looking at my phone," "I fell asleep," or "I am running late for work" are all statements that will get reported to the judge in court. The judge will then take those statements into account as evidence that you were in fact reckless driving.

Regardless of the type of Reckless Driving charge you are facing, it is important to respectfully and specifically tell the police officer that you "invoke your right and privilege against self-incrimination and do not wish to answer any questions or make any statements." The 5th Amendment of the U.S. Constitution states that you have the right to remain silent. Even if you believe that you are 100% innocent, do not answer any questions or make any statements. The importance and significance of not answering any questions or making any statements is that you are not providing the police officer with chatter to use as ammo against you in court. Also, the mere act of you invoking your right and privilege against self-incrimination cannot be used against you as evidence of your guilt.

Also, in my experience I have seen that being a jerk to the police officer does more harm than good. If there is a problem, let an attorney fix it in court. Even if you believe that you are 100% innocent, you should not try to fix the problem on the side of the road, even if you are a police officer or attorney yourself. Because when you are on the side of the road, you are in the police officer's territory — but when you are in court, the police officer is in the attorney's territory.

This would apply to anyone charged with any criminal offense, even outside of Reckless Driving.

CHAPTER 3

FLOW OF A RECKLESS DRIVING CASE IN VIRGINIA

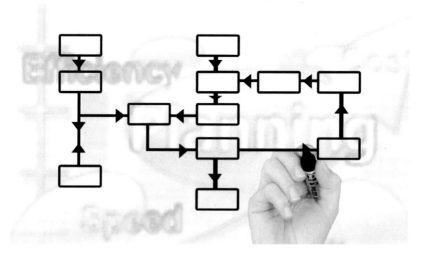

Reckless Driving cases are heard in the General District Court ("GDC") in the city or county where the alleged offense occurred. However, if you were 17 years old or younger at the time of the alleged offense, your Reckless Driving case will be heard in the Juvenile and Domestic Relations Court ("JDRC") in the city or county where the alleged offense occurred. A parent or legal guardian of a juvenile driver charged with Reckless Driving in the JDRC is usually required to appear in court along with the juvenile.

If you want to view your case information online, you may do so by visiting:

http://www.courts.state.va.us/caseinfo/home.html.

First, while on the court website, click the tab on the left side of the screen that says Case Status and Information. Second, click the tab that says General District Court. Third, click the tab that says Case Information. Fourth, accept the Terms and Conditions of Use by clicking the tab that says Accept. Fifth, select the specific court in which you are charged. Sixth, underneath Traffic/Criminal, click the tab that says Name Search. Finally, enter your last and first name and then click the tab that says Search. This will pull up your case information.

If you cannot find your case information, it is possible that your name was misspelled when it was entered into the court's website. In that situation, try locating your case under a Hearing Date Search. If that still does not work, wait a few business days and try again because the police officer may have not yet filed your paperwork with the court or the court clerk may have not yet entered your case into the court's website.

Notably, due to privacy laws, you cannot view case information online for cases in the JDRC.

When Will I Have My First Court Date?

Your court date and time should be written on the top left-hand corner of your ticket.

You must appear in court for a Reckless Driving ticket in Virginia. Some courts in Virginia will allow you to stay at home if you hire an attorney and if your case has no realistic likelihood of you receiving a jail sentence.

For the average Reckless Driving case, there is usually just one court date, which is called your "trial" date. The trial date is usually set 4 to 8 weeks after the date of the alleged offense.

However, if your case has a realistic likelihood of you receiving a jail sentence, the police officer or judge may give you two court dates. In that situation, your first court date is called your "arraignment" date and your second court date is called your "trial" date.

The arraignment date is usually set 4 to 8 weeks after the date of the alleged offense. The arraignment date is simply a preliminary, housekeeping-type of hearing where the judge is only going to formally advise you of your specific charge, ask about your plan for obtaining an attorney, and set your case for a trial date.

The trial date is usually set 4 to 8 weeks after the arraignment date. The trial date is the actual hearing where the action happens. This is the hearing where you enter a plea of not guilty, no contest, or guilty and the judge hears the evidence and renders a verdict. It is the day your case will be resolved and finished.

What Can I Expect The Day Of Court?

If this is your first time going to court, you are probably feeling nervous and stressed out about it. This is because you do not know what to expect. Allow me to alleviate your concerns by explaining what to expect in court.

The address for your court is located on the top left-hand corner of your ticket. Plan to arrive to court 15 – 20 minutes early. Expect to be in court between 30 minutes to 2 hours. Dress as nicely as possible. I have heard judges say that dressing nicely shows respect for the court and shows that you are taking your case seriously. Most, but not all, courts in Virginia will prohibit you from bringing in your cell phone and smart watch. You will be required to walk through a metal detector to be screened for illegal contraband, including a cell phone or smart watch.

Once inside the courthouse, locate your specific courtroom. There should be either a paper or electronic docket posted in the hallway of the courthouse that will tell you your specific courtroom. After you figure that out, go inside your specific courtroom, have a seat, and wait quietly for the judge to call your case.

When the judge calls your case, walk up to the judge's bench or the counsel table. Keep your hands out of your pockets at all times and do not chew gum. Conduct yourself properly and refer to the judge as "Your Honor." The judge will first ask you how you wish to plead: not guilty, no contest, or guilty. How to plead will depend on the specific facts of your case.

A plea of "not guilty" means that you are saying you are innocent of the offense or have a defense in your case.

A plea of "no contest" means that you are not saying you are guilty, but are saying the evidence is sufficient to find you guilty of the offense.

A plea of "guilty" means that you are saying you are guilty of the offense.

The decision how to plead must be made on a case-by-case basis. Every case is different. Some cases may be better to plead not guilty, while others may be better to plead guilty.

How you decide to plead will determine the manner in which your trial is conducted.

If you decide to plead "not guilty," you will have a full blown trial in your case. There will be a formal presentation of the evidence. As soon as you tell the judge that you are pleading not guilty, the judge will swear-in all witnesses that intend to testify at your trial. You can ask the judge to separate those witnesses so they do not piggyback off each other's testimony. The first witnesses to testify will be the police officer and then any witnesses for the police officer. Each witness will tell the judge what they personally observed. Then, you will have the opportunity to ask those witnesses questions (this is called cross examination). After the police officer and all of his or her witnesses have finished testifying, it is now your turn to make any motions, raise any defenses, and put on evidence, but you do not have to. At this point in time, you can testify and tell the judge your side of the story, but you do not have to. The 5th Amendment of the U.S. Constitution states that you have the right to remain silent. Also, the mere act of you invoking your right to remain silent cannot be used against you as evidence of your guilt. If you choose to testify and thus waive your right to remain silent, be aware that the judge or prosecutor (if there is one) is now allowed to ask you questions and you will be required to answer their questions honestly. You can also have any witnesses on your side testify, but you do not have to. You can also play video footage and audio recordings and show the judge pictures, but you do not have to. After you and all of your witnesses have finished testifying, you can now make any final motions, raise any final defenses, and provide a closing argument to the judge, but you do not have to. Next, the judge will render a verdict (i.e., make a decision) regarding whether or not you are guilty of the charge. This will mark the end of the "guilt or innocence phase of trial." If you are found not guilty, your charge will be immediately dropped and you can turn around and leave the court unscathed. On the other hand, if you are found guilty, your case will move forward to the sentencing phase of trial. The "sentencing phase of trial" is the point in time where the judge determines an appropriate punishment for you. This is where you will be able to tell the judge who you are as a person and you can offer into evidence (i.e., hand the judge) your mitigating documents and respectfully request that the judge dismiss or reduce your Reckless Driving charge to a lesser, non-criminal charge. You are not required to say anything or provide any documents to the judge. The judge will then determine and impose your punishment. After the judge imposes your punishment, you will be required to stop by the court clerk to obtain all of your paperwork and information related to your fines and court costs. When you are done with the clerk, you can leave the court.

If you decide to plead "no contest" or "guilty," you will not have a full blown trial in your case. Instead, your case will proceed directly to the sentencing phase of trial. In this situation, there will not be a formal presentation of the evidence. By pleading no contest or guilty, you are forfeiting your right to challenge the evidence. This means that none of the witnesses will testify and you will not have an opportunity to question them. This also means that you will not have the opportunity to present any evidence or raise any defenses in your case. The judge might, however, ask the police officer to give an informal summary of the facts of your case so the judge can determine how to punish you. After the police officer gives the judge a summary of your case, you will be able to tell the judge who you are as a person and you can offer into evidence (i.e., hand the judge) your mitigating documents and respectfully request that the judge dismiss or reduce your Reckless Driving charge to a lesser, non-criminal charge. You are not required to say anything or provide any documents to the judge. The judge will then determine and impose your punishment. After the judge imposes your punishment, you will be required to stop by the court clerk to obtain all of your paperwork and information related to your fines and court costs. When you are done with the clerk, you can leave the court.

Is It Possible To Have A Reckless Driving Charge Reduced To A Lesser Charge?

It is definitely possible to have a Reckless Driving charge reduced to a lesser, non-criminal charge. The judge has the same mentality as a parent. The judge is basically a parent to society. If you take the right approach with the judge to mitigate your case, the judge may reduce your Reckless Driving charge to a lesser, non-criminal charge.

To be clear, "mitigate" or "mitigating" in the context of a Reckless Driving case means to provide positive facts and documents to the judge to make both you and your case look better.

As far as how to do that, different judges like to see and hear different mitigating facts about you and your case, but ultimately, there are some commonalities in regard to the mitigating documents judges want to see. It is important to note that judges do not just handout a reduced charge – you have to work for and earn a reduced charge. This means that you must show the judge you are remorseful, understand the seriousness of the offense, and are not going to recidivate and do it again.

If you can show the judge that, the judge will have a peace of mind in knowing that you have learned your lesson. As a result, the judge will show mercy and leniency toward you in the form of using their discretionary judicial powers to reduce your Reckless Driving charge to a lesser, non-criminal charge.

You do have to provide certain mitigating documents to the judge in order to show the judge you are remorseful, understand the seriousness of the offense, and are not going to recidivate and do it again. That would include you obtaining <u>before</u> <u>court</u> the <u>original</u> version of the following mitigating documents:

(i)   **Driving Record** – Obtain the most formal or legitimate version of your driving record from the DMV that accounts for the past 5 years in time from the date of the alleged offense. This typically costs between $0 - $30 depending on your home state's DMV.

(ii) **Driver Improvement Program** – Obtain a certificate of completion of a DMV approved 8 hour driver improvement program. This is sometimes called a "traffic school" or "defensive driving course" (they all mean the same thing). This typically costs between $30 - $75 depending on where you go. You may complete this program in any city in any state. If you are 20 years old or older, you may complete this program in-person or online. If you are 19 years old or younger, you must complete this program in-person only. Either way, your local phone book, DMV website, or a Google search will reveal that there are many DMV approved 8 hour driver improvement programs wherever you live. Indicate that you are taking the program for "voluntary" or "point-reduction" purposes. This is not "court ordered" or "court required." Notably, you are ineligible to take a driver improvement program if you are a CDL holder because there is both a federal and state law barring CDL holders from getting credit in court for completing a driver improvement program. This is true whether you were driving a commercial vehicle or a personal vehicle when you received your ticket.

(iii)   **Speedometer Calibration** – If you are charged with Reckless Driving By Speed, obtain a notarized speedometer calibration report for the vehicle you were driving when you received your Reckless Driving ticket. This is the best thing that you can do for this type of case hands down. This typically costs between $50 - $150 depending on where you go. A "speedometer calibration" is an accuracy check from a mechanic that shows whether or not the speedometer in your vehicle is displaying an accurate reading. During the performance of the speedometer calibration, the mechanic will not fix, repair, or replace anything in your vehicle. Instead, the mechanic is simply going to perform a computer diagnostic test to determine the accuracy of your speedometer. If your speedometer is not accurate, your "notarized speedometer calibration report" will tell you how much your speedometer is off by. For example, your speedometer may be reading 3 mph slower than your actual speed. Therefore, when your speedometer indicates that you are driving 75 mph, you are actually driving 78 mph. As a result, the judge will not fault you for that discrepancy. Ideally, you want your notarized speedometer calibration report to show that your speedometer is reading slower than your actual speed.

(iv) **Military Annual Performance Evaluation** – If you are in the military, obtain your most recent annual performance evaluation from the military.

(v) **College Transcripts or Class Schedule** – If you are a college student and have a cumulative GPA of a 3.0 or higher, obtain your unofficial college transcripts. If you have a cumulative GPA of a 2.9 or lower, obtain your current class schedule.

(vi) **Community Service** – If your case has a realistic likelihood of you receiving a jail sentence, obtain a letter from a legitimate non-profit or charitable organization that is written on their letterhead and confirms you have completed between 10 to 50 hours of unpaid community service at their organization. To determine if your case has a realistic likelihood of you receiving a jail sentence, please refer to page 78. You must not get paid or receive credit at any school or job for your completion of this community service.

(vii) **Typed Essay** – If you are 19 years old or younger, type a 2-paragraph essay on what constitutes the specific type of Reckless Driving charge you are facing and the consequences of a Reckless Driving conviction. This book could be a helpful resource here.

These are things that I recommend my clients do before court because it shows the judge that a lesson has been learned from this experience. It shows the judge that you understand and respect the seriousness of it and that you are not going to do it again.

The illustration on the next page shows the most common charges a judge could reduce your Reckless Driving ticket to.

HIERARCHY OF MAJOR TRAFFIC OFFENSES IN VIRGINIA

RECKLESS DRIVING

- Class 1 misdemeanor criminal offense
- Potential jail sentence and driver's license suspension
- Adds 6 demerit points to your driving record and the conviction appears on your driving record for 11 years*

SPEEDING 20 MPH+ OVER

- Non-criminal offense
- Adds 6 demerit points to your driving record and the conviction appears on your driving record for 5 years*

SPEEDING 10-19 MPH OVER

- Non-criminal offense
- Adds 4 demerit points to your driving record and the conviction appears on your driving record for 5 years*

SPEEDING 1-9 MPH OVER

- Non-criminal offense
- Adds 3 demerit points to your driving record and the conviction appears on your driving record for 5 years*

IMPROPER DRIVING

- Non-criminal offense
- Adds 3 demerit points to your driving record and the conviction appears on your driving record for 3 years*

DEFECTIVE / IMPROPER EQUIPMENT

- Non-criminal offense
- No demerit points added to your driving record, but the conviction appears on your driving record for 3 years*

NOT GUILTY / DISMISSAL

- No conviction whatsoever
- No demerit points

*NOTE: If you have a driver's license from a state other than Virginia, it is up to your home state's Department of Motor Vehicles regarding: (i) whether or not the conviction will appear on your driving record; (ii) the amount of demerit points that will be added to your driving record; and (iii) the length of time the conviction will appear on your driving record.

CHAPTER 4

IMPORTANT EVIDENCE FOR MY RECKLESS DRIVING DEFENSE

The best way to prepare evidence to fight, challenge, or contest a Reckless Driving ticket at trial is to record video footage and play that video footage in court. Video footage is the best way to preserve evidence and it can help you win a case regardless of the type of Reckless Driving charge you are facing.

Typically, a dash camera — that is, a video camera mounted on the dashboard of your car — will not show

61

your speedometer reading because it will only capture video footage outside your front windshield. Therefore, to capture the best video footage, a video camera should be safely mounted in a position where it captures both your speedometer reading and outside your front windshield. If you can capture this video footage, it could negate any allegation that you were speeding. It would also be helpful in this situation if you obtain a notarized speedometer calibration report to prove that your speedometer was displaying an accurate speed at the time your video footage was recorded.

If you do not have a mounted video camera in your car, you can use a cell phone to record video footage as long as you are doing it safely and without distracting your driving or interaction with the police officer (or you can have a passenger record the video). There is no law that prohibits you from video recording the police. Police officers are not required to video record on their end. Therefore, police officers typically do not video record Reckless Driving cases. Although, police officers will video record in more serious criminal cases. Nonetheless, you can video record on your end without being a jerk about it to the police officer, or any other witness.

If you are hesitant to video record on the side of the road or play video footage in court, you can at least pull out a cell phone and audio record. It is ideal if you can capture video footage, but if capturing that will create problems or if you are worried about pointing your cell phone at the police officer or witness in order to capture video, audio only is fine. To audio record only, turn on your cell phone's video camera or audio-recording app, press the record button, and place your phone face-down on the dashboard or in another location. Even audio recordings can help you win your trial because a lot of times a police officer or witness will make statements on the side of the road that they do not make in court. This calls into question their credibility and recollection of events.

For example, a police officer on the side of the road can say "Well, I couldn't get a clear speed on you, but I think you were going 89 mph," but when the police officer gets to court, he or she will say your speed with much more confidence. In such cases, video footage and audio recordings can help show the judge or jury that the police officer's evidence is shaky or questionable. This could create reasonable doubt in your trial and get your Reckless Driving charge dismissed.

If you were in an accident, not only should you record video footage, you should also take pictures of the scene of the accident from multiple angles. Take pictures in color and in high-definition. Take pictures of all damages caused to all vehicles and property. Take pictures of all bodily injuries. Take pictures of the geography of the landscape. Make sure the pictures are taken as soon as possible after the accident. Ideally, you want the pictures to show the lighting, road, and weather conditions as they were at the time of the accident. You want the pictures to show the curvature and slope of the road.

If you were accused of speeding, take a picture of the posted speed limit sign near the location of the alleged offense. The location of the alleged offense is not the same location where you were pulled over by the police officer. The bottom right-hand corner of your ticket will tell you the location of the alleged offense. If a police officer says that you were driving 75 mph in a posted 55 mph zone, but you think that you were actually in a posted 65 mph or 70 mph zone, go back to the location of the alleged offense and record video footage or take a picture of the nearest posted speed limit sign. Sometimes the difficulty with this is that you do not always know exactly and precisely where you were located when the police officer determined your alleged speed. Just because you were pulled over at a certain location does not mean that you were speeding at that same location. Perhaps the police officer clocked your speed 45 seconds or 3 minutes before you were pulled over.

In my experience, video footage, audio recordings, and pictures have helped me win a lot of cases.

CHAPTER 5

WHEN DOES THE PROSECUTION OFFER A PLEA DEAL?

In Virginia, prosecutors are not always involved in Reckless Driving cases. It depends on the particular city or county in which you are charged. If there is a prosecutor involved in your case, he or she may offer you a plea deal if there are enough mitigating facts in your case. For starters, the cleaner your driving and criminal record, the more likely the prosecutor is going to offer you a favorable plea deal. Whereas the more convictions you have on your driving and criminal record, the less likely the prosecutor is going to offer you a favorable plea deal. Moreover, if you obtain the right mitigating documents before court, it will persuade the prosecutor to offer you a favorable plea deal.

Frankly speaking, prosecutors have an incentive to offer you a plea deal because it makes their job easier. It is one less trial for them. From a prosecutor's standpoint, it lightens their load because they handle a high volume of cases on a daily basis and they are pressured to plow through their dockets in court as quickly as possible. So a plea deal could benefit both you and the prosecutor.

If there are bad or aggravating facts in your case, or if you have a bad driving or criminal record, a prosecutor may not want to offer you a plea deal, but may want to purposefully go to trial so the judge can decide your case. Ultimately, it depends on your driving and criminal record, the specific facts of your case, and the amount of mitigating documents you have obtained before court.

What Might A Plea Deal Look Like?

Every plea deal is different. A plea deal will always be determined on a case by case basis. It will be specifically tailored to the individual person and the particular facts of the case. There is no "one-size-fits-all" plea deal or outcome.

Conversation With Your Client When Deciding Whether To Take A Case To Trial Or Accept A Plea Deal/Plead Guilty

The conversation varies depending on the case. Any person, in any type of criminal case, Reckless Driving or Murder, has only two options: go to trial or accept a plea deal/plead guilty.

With that being said, the conversation with my client about whether to go to trial or accept a plea deal/plead guilty really hinges on the particular facts of the case and whether or not I think the evidence can prove beyond a reasonable doubt that my client is guilty. Moreover, there are technical defenses to a Reckless Driving charge that can result in a dismissal of the charge even if my client is actually guilty of it.

If the evidence cannot prove beyond a reasonable doubt that my client is guilty of Reckless Driving (or if there is a technical defense), then I advise my clients to plead not guilty and go to trial. A "trial" is a contested hearing where the evidence is formally presented to a judge or jury. A trial is a hearing where you fight, challenge, or contest a criminal charge. This is what you see in movies. At trial, if the evidence can prove beyond a reasonable doubt that you are guilty of the alleged offense, the judge or jury will find you guilty and convict you. On the other hand, if the evidence cannot prove beyond a reasonable doubt that you are guilty of the alleged offense (or if there is a technical defense), the judge or jury will find you not guilty and acquit you.

But if the evidence is pretty solid and stacked against my client, then I — as a last resort — advise my clients to accept a plea deal or plead no contest or guilty as it will ensure a better outcome in their case.

For example, maybe there is an accident case that involves a driver who had a seizure while driving and hit a tree. When the police officer arrived at the scene, the driver was passed out behind the wheel. The driver did not make any statements to the police officer. There were no witnesses. The police officer does not know what happened and decided to charge the driver with Reckless Driving Failure To Maintain Control. In that situation, I would advise the driver to plead not guilty and go to trial to contest any allegation of reckless driving.

The other side of the coin is if the police officer has his or her ducks in a row and can prove the case with actual evidence of reckless driving, such as evidence of speed, erratic or crazy driving, distracted driving, impaired driving, impatient driving, or risk-taking driving. In that situation, it would be better not to go to trial, but to accept a plea deal or plead no contest or guilty because by doing that, you are removing certain risks from the table that are attached to going to trial.

This is why I make it a habit of speaking with the police officer before going in front of the judge as it allows me to get a feel for whether or not the police officer's evidence can prove beyond a reasonable doubt that my client is guilty and whether or not there are any technical defenses in the case.

CHAPTER 6

DEFENSE STRATEGIES IN RECKLESS DRIVING CASES

There are 3 ways to defeat a Reckless Driving ticket.

The first way to defeat a Reckless Driving ticket is to determine, either before or during trial, whether or not the police officer can prove beyond a reasonable doubt that you are guilty of Reckless Driving.

In America, there is a presumption of innocence for any type of criminal charge, including a Reckless Driving ticket. This means that you are considered innocent until proven guilty. To be proven guilty, the police officer must prove beyond a reasonable doubt that you have in fact committed the alleged offense.

To "prove beyond a reasonable doubt" means the police officer's evidence must be strong enough to remove any reasonable doubt in the mind of the judge or jury that you are guilty of the crime charged.

If there is any reasonable doubt remaining, the charge must be dropped.

To make this determination, it is important to examine and scrutinize all video footage, audio recordings, and pictures. In addition, it is important to examine and scrutinize what the police officer and witnesses say and testify to in court. Perhaps the police officer and witnesses make inconsistent statements or their level of confidence and certainty is questionable.

A lot of times in an accident case, the police officer or witness did not see the driver's driving behavior, but rather showed up after the accident happened. Thus, the police officer or witness did not personally see anything and cannot tell the judge anything about the driver's driving behavior. If those witnesses are not able to say anything about the driver's driving behavior at trial, this can create reasonable doubt in the case as there is no evidence of reckless driving.

Furthermore, if there are witnesses that stopped to talk to the police officer, the police officer needs to subpoena those witnesses to physically come to court and testify under oath as to what they observed. The police officer is not allowed to tell the judge or jury what the witnesses said or wrote down on the side of the road because those statements are considered inadmissible "hearsay." If those witnesses are not present in court — and since their out-of-court statements are inadmissible at trial because they are hearsay — this can create reasonable doubt in the case as there is no evidence of reckless driving.

The bottom line is that if the police officer cannot prove beyond a reasonable doubt that you are guilty of the alleged offense, you will be found not guilty and your charge will be dropped. On the other hand, if the police officer can prove beyond a reasonable doubt that you are guilty of the alleged offense, move on to the second way to defeat a Reckless Driving ticket.

The second way to defeat a Reckless Driving ticket is to determine, either before or during the trial, if there are any technical defenses in your case.

A "technical defense" means that due to a technicality in the case, the charge must be dropped even if you are actually guilty of it.

To make this determination, it is important to examine and scrutinize the entire process and procedure used by the police officer in your case. Technical defenses must be timely executed and properly argued at trial. If not, they are deemed to be waived.

There are several technical defenses to a Reckless Driving ticket. These technical defenses include, but are not limited to, whether or not the police officer can prove that the court in which you are charged has proper jurisdiction of the case, that the statute of limitations to initiate a Reckless Driving charge has not yet expired, that you were driving on a "highway," that the police officer's radar gun, laser gun, or police car's speedometer has been properly calibrated for its accuracy within 6 months before the offense date, and that the procedure used to investigate your case complies with proper police procedure, etc.

In addition, it is important to examine and scrutinize the actual ticket the police officer gave you because sometimes there are technical or clerical mistakes on your ticket that can result in your charge being dropped. It would be a good idea to provide your attorney with the original version of your ticket, or at least a photocopy of it.

The bottom line is that if there is a technical defense in your case, you will be found not guilty and your charge will be dropped. On the other hand, if there is not a technical defense in your case, move on to the third way to defeat a Reckless Driving ticket.

The third way to defeat a Reckless Driving ticket is to damage-control your case at the sentencing phase of trial.

To "damage-control" your case means to try and convince the judge to show mercy and leniency toward you.

To do this, wait until the sentencing phase of trial —
which occurs at the end of your trial immediately after the
judge has determined you are guilty of Reckless Driving —
and offer into evidence (i.e., hand the judge) your mitigating
documents and respectfully request that the judge dismiss or
reduce your Reckless Driving charge to a lesser, non-criminal
charge. You can also do this outright by accepting a plea deal
or by pleading no contest or guilty at the very beginning of
your trial. Either way, you must obtain before court the
mitigating documents I have outlined on pages 55 - 58.

CHAPTER 7

WHAT IS THE PUNISHMENT FOR A RECKLESS DRIVING CONVICTION?

It is simply up to the judge or jury how to punish you. As long as the judge or jury works within the statutory guidelines permitted for a class 1 misdemeanor conviction, the punishment will be upheld as valid. Since a Reckless Driving ticket is a class 1 misdemeanor, the judge or jury can impose a jail sentence of up to 12 months, a fine of up to $2,500, and a suspension of your driver's license for up to 6 months.

If you are not licensed in Virginia, the judge or jury can "suspend your privilege to drive in Virginia" for up to 6 months. Most likely, that will reciprocate over to your home state. This means that your home state may honor the suspension of your privilege to drive in Virginia and, in turn, implement a full-blown suspension of your driver's license across all 50 states.

Will I Go To Jail If I Am Convicted Of Reckless Driving?

In most cases, people do not go to jail if they are convicted of Reckless Driving. However, some cases do carry a realistic likelihood of a jail sentence.

Your case has "a realistic likelihood of you receiving a jail sentence" if you have a terrible driving or criminal record, have been accused of driving 30 mph or more above the posted speed limit, have been accused of driving 90 mph or higher regardless of the posted speed limit, were disrespectful and uncooperative to the police officer, or caused injuries to another person.

Your presiding judge also matters. Some judges are more lenient than others when it comes to imposing a jail sentence.

If you feel that you fall into this category, do not worry. Most jail sentences I see are way below the maximum amount of 12 months. In cases where a jail sentence is actually imposed, the jail sentence is usually between 1 – 30 days, which can be served on the weekends. If you want to avoid or minimize any potential jail time you may receive, this book explains the many things you need to do.

Will I Lose My Driver's License If I Am Convicted Of Reckless Driving?

In most cases, people do not lose their driver's license if they are convicted of Reckless Driving. However, some cases do carry a realistic likelihood of a driver's license suspension.

Your case has "a realistic likelihood of a driver's license suspension" if you have a terrible driving or criminal record, have been accused of driving 30 mph or more above the posted speed limit, have been accused of driving 90 mph or higher regardless of the posted speed limit, were disrespectful and uncooperative to the police officer, or caused injuries to another person.

Your presiding judge also matters. Some judges are more lenient than others when it comes to imposing a driver's license suspension.

If you feel that you fall into this category, do not worry. In cases where a driver's license suspension is actually imposed, the period of suspension is usually for 1, 2, 3, or 6 months and the judge will usually grant you a "restricted driver's license," which allows you to drive to and from school, work, jail (if any), a place of religious worship, and medical appointments. If you want to avoid or minimize any potential driver's license suspension you may receive, this book explains the many things you need to do.

How Much Will I Pay In Fines And Court Costs If I Am Convicted Of Reckless Driving?

Most fines I see are way below the maximum amount of $2,500. It ultimately depends on the type of charge you are convicted of. Generally speaking, if you are convicted of any type of Reckless Driving charge, you can expect to pay the court anywhere between $250 - $1,000 in combined fines and court costs. However, if you are convicted of a lesser, non-criminal charge, you can expect to pay the court anywhere between $50 - $500 in combined fines and court costs.

Regardless, your fines and court costs are typically due to the court within 30 - 90 calendar days after the date of your conviction.

What Are The Long-Term Consequences Of A Reckless Driving Conviction?

The long-term consequences of a Reckless Driving conviction are that you will have a permanent criminal conviction that cannot be removed from your criminal record. You would have to disclose that criminal conviction on job applications, various license applications, and security clearance applications if the application asks if you have ever been convicted of a misdemeanor.

That conviction could prevent you from obtaining certain jobs, or in the alternative, make you a less-attractive candidate for certain jobs. That conviction could prevent you from obtaining a CDL, and if you already have one, it could be revoked.

If I Take My Case To Trial And Lose, Will I Face A Stiffer Punishment Than If I Had Taken A Plea Deal / Plead Guilty?

If you take your case to trial and lose, it is certainly possible that you could face a stiffer punishment, but that depends on a variety of factors including, but not limited to, your driving and criminal record, the specific facts of your case, the amount of mitigating documents you have obtained before court, and your particular judge. This is a decision that should be thoroughly discussed with an attorney because it is highly fact-specific and the smallest detail in your case matters. In fact, the smallest detail could be a game changer.

Usually, most judges will not punish you for going to trial. However, if there are bad or aggravating facts in your case, you might get a stiffer punishment going to trial and losing than if you had just outright taken a plea deal or pled guilty.

Is It Possible To Appeal A Reckless Driving Conviction In Virginia?

If you are unhappy with the outcome of your case in either the GDC or the JDRC, you may appeal your case up to the Circuit Court in the city or county where the alleged offense occurred.

The Circuit Court is a higher up court. Your appeal would be heard in the Circuit Court and is considered an "appeal de novo." An appeal de novo gives you a clean slate and a new beginning with your case, allowing you to start over from scratch. In some jurisdictions, you can actually obtain a better outcome of your case on appeal.

You have 10 calendar days from the date of your conviction to note your appeal with the GDC or JDRC, respectively. The date of your conviction is considered day 1, and weekends and holidays are included in this 10-day period. On day 11, it is too late to note your appeal.

By virtue of you noting your appeal, your Reckless Driving conviction and punishment from the GDC or JDRC will be erased and your Reckless Driving charge will revert back to being a "pending charge." Therefore, you will not have a conviction on your driving and criminal record if and when you note your appeal.

If you do appeal your case, there is usually just one court date in the Circuit Court, which is called your "appeal-trial" date. The appeal-trial date is usually set 4 to 8 weeks after the date of your conviction in the GDC or JDRC.

However, if your case has a realistic likelihood of you receiving a jail sentence or if the Circuit Court judge wants to control the volume of its docket, the judge may give you two court dates. In that situation, your first court date would be your "arraignment" date and your second court date would be your "appeal-trial" date.

The arraignment date is usually set 4 to 8 weeks after the date of your conviction in the GDC or JDRC. Sometimes your arraignment date in the Circuit Court is called a "docket call" date. The arraignment or docket call date is simply a preliminary, housekeeping-type of hearing where the Circuit Court judge is only going to formally advise you of your specific charge, ask about your plan for obtaining an attorney, and set your case for an appeal-trial date.

The appeal-trial date is usually set 4 to 8 weeks after the arraignment date. The appeal-trial date is the actual hearing where the action happens. This is the hearing where you enter a plea of not guilty, no contest, or guilty and the judge or jury hears the evidence and renders a verdict.

Notably, you have the right to have a jury trial in the Circuit Court for a Reckless Driving ticket. This is a trial where a jury of 7 of your peers — not a judge — must decide whether or not you are guilty of Reckless Driving. It is not possible to have a jury trial in the GDC or JDRC. The decision, however, to have a jury trial in the Circuit Court should be something that is thoroughly discussed with an attorney as there are many pros and cons to a jury trial.

The appeal in the Circuit Court is usually your last bite at the apple. Technically, the Court of Appeals of Virginia and the Supreme Court of Virginia are higher up courts that could hear criminal appeals, but in reality, those courts will not hear Reckless Driving appeals unless there was a severe legal error in the Circuit Court. In my experience and that of other attorneys, most Reckless Driving cases will not make it past the Circuit Court. Thus, it is best to have the mentality that the Circuit Court is your last bite at the apple.

CHAPTER 8

WHAT SHOULD I EXPECT FROM MY CAR INSURANCE AND THE DMV?

If you are convicted of a Reckless Driving ticket it will impact your car insurance more than a normal speeding ticket. As an attorney, I can only say that a conviction of Reckless Driving will cause an increase in your car insurance premium, but I cannot provide a specific dollar amount because that is up to your specific car insurance carrier. If you are under someone else's car insurance policy, your conviction of Reckless Driving will cause an increase in that person's car insurance premium.

If you are convicted of a Reckless Driving ticket it will impact you with the Department of Motor Vehicles ("DMV") more than a normal speeding ticket. The Virginia DMV will put the conviction on your Virginia driving record. If you are not licensed in Virginia, the conviction may likely show up on your driving record in your home state. In America, 45 states are participants to an agreement called the Driver's License Compact ("DLC"). The DLC is an agreement between 45 states where each state has agreed to share driving record information with each other and treat out-of-state traffic offenses as if they occurred in the home state.

For example, let's say you are licensed in New Jersey and are convicted of a Reckless Driving ticket in Virginia. Since New Jersey is one of the 45 states that is a participant to the DLC, your Reckless Driving conviction in Virginia will appear on your New Jersey driving record. This is because the New Jersey DMV is going to treat the offense as if it happened in New Jersey and thus add the conviction and demerit points to your New Jersey driving record.

Therefore, even if you are licensed in a different state, for the most part, your home state's DMV is going to honor and accept the Reckless Driving conviction from Virginia and treat it as if it happened in your home state.

Notably, if you start racking up too many demerit points on your driving record, your DMV will either put you on a probationary period or administratively suspend your driver's license.

How Long Will A Reckless Driving Conviction Stay On My Criminal And Driving Record?

A Reckless Driving conviction will stay on your criminal record for the rest of your life and it cannot be removed, expunged, sealed, hidden, or erased from your criminal record no matter what.

The length of time a Reckless Driving conviction will stay on your driving record depends on the state in which you are licensed.

If you are licensed in Virginia, a Reckless Driving conviction will add 6 demerit points to your driving record and the conviction will remain on your driving record for 11 years.

If you are licensed outside of Virginia and in one of the 45 states that is a participant to the DLC, it would be up to your home state's DMV regarding how many demerit points to assign to your driving record and the length of time the conviction will appear on your driving record.

If you are licensed outside of Virginia and in one of the 5 states that is not a participant to the DLC, the conviction will not appear on your driving record, nor will you receive any demerit points. The 5 states that do not participate in the DLC are Georgia, Massachusetts, Michigan, Tennessee, and Wisconsin. However, that does not mean you should just walk away and ignore your Reckless Driving ticket because the conviction can still appear on your criminal record regardless of the DLC.

CHAPTER 9

BEST TIME TO FIND A RECKLESS DRIVING ATTORNEY

The best time to find an experienced Reckless Driving attorney to represent you is as soon as possible because it takes time to build a defense and obtain the right mitigating documents for your case.

As far as building a defense for your case, you and your attorney may need to act quickly and interview witnesses while the events are still fresh in their mind, obtain your medical documents, properly request video footage before it gets erased, or capture pictures of your wrecked car before it gets hauled off to the junkyard, etc.

As far as obtaining the right mitigating documents for your case, you and your attorney may need to act quickly before your ability to obtain these mitigating documents vanishes. For example, if you were charged with Reckless Driving By Speed and you were driving a rental car during the alleged offense, you should definitely get a speedometer calibration done on that car. Your attorney can help you find a proper mechanic that can perform a speedometer calibration and provide you with a proper notarized speedometer calibration report. The problem is that if you have already returned that rental car, you will not be able to get a speedometer calibration done. Without a speedometer calibration, you will not be able to obtain the best-of-the-best outcome of your case.

The bottom line is the sooner you contact an attorney, the sooner you and your attorney have time to gather and preserve evidence that may be beneficial to your case.

Important Information And Documents To Share With My Attorney

If you have a Reckless Driving ticket, you should provide the following information and documents to your attorney:

(i)   Your full name, age, and city and state of residence;

(ii)   The original version of your ticket or a photocopy of it;

(iii)   A thorough description of the facts of your case;

(iv)   A thorough description of all statements you made to the police officer and witnesses;

(v)   A list of all known witnesses to include their full name and complete home or work address;

(vi)   A thorough description of all statements the police officer and witnesses made to you;

(vii)   All video footage, audio recordings, and pictures of the alleged offense;

(viii) Whether or not you have any previous convictions on your driving and criminal records;

(ix)   Whether or not you were on probation at the time of the alleged offense;

(x)   Whether or not you have any other pending traffic or criminal charges;

(xi) Whether or not you are in the military;

(xii) Whether or not you are in college;

(xiii) Your U.S. immigration status in America;

(xiv) Any bad or avoid dates you may have for appearing in court (these are not guaranteed to be avoided);

(xv) Anything positive that can be said about you; and

(xvi) The mitigating documents I have outlined on pages 55 – 58.

What Do You Tell People Who Just Want To Plead Guilty And Get It Over With?

I tell people who want to outright plead guilty to a Reckless Driving ticket because they want to get it over with to not do it.

The reason why is because it is possible to beat these charges and obtain a not guilty verdict or at the very least, have your charge reduced to a lesser, non-criminal offense even if you are actually guilty of your Reckless Driving ticket. There are a lot of defenses, especially technical defenses, attached to a Reckless Driving ticket. The value of an attorney is that the attorney knows all of the defenses and how to best approach your particular judge.

CHAPTER 10

SHOULD I HIRE AN ATTORNEY TO DEFEND MY CASE?

It is certainly smart to hire an attorney to defend you because there are many defensive tactics that go into defeating a Reckless Driving ticket.

In order to effectively conduct a trial in a criminal case, such as Reckless Driving, you must be familiar with multiple areas of law. This includes Criminal Law, Criminal Procedure, Constitutional Law, The Rules Of Evidence, and The Rules Of The Supreme Court Of

Virginia. The average person is not familiar with these areas of law.

There are many defenses that go into a Reckless Driving case and there are many pitfalls to avoid at trial. An attorney has the specific education and training to effectively conduct a trial. An attorney knows how to ask the right questions during your trial in order to find reasonable doubt in your case. Moreover, the average person is not familiar with the technical defenses in a Reckless Driving case. An attorney knows how to catch and argue these technical defenses at trial. An attorney is also a zealous advocate for you who knows the right approach to take in order to damage-control your case in front of your particular judge. I see a lot of people without attorneys in court who throw dirt on the police officer or say the wrong things to the judge and that actually backfires against them.

Public Defenders Versus Private Attorneys

Public defenders are usually not appointed on Reckless Driving cases unless your case has a realistic likelihood of you receiving a jail sentence and your income is at or below 125% of the federal poverty guidelines. Your "income" includes your personal income, your spouse's income, your household size, the value of your assets, and the amount of money in your bank accounts and on-hand. To see if you qualify for a public defender in your case, you must appear in court and ask the judge to screen you for a public defender.

If you choose to hire an attorney for a Reckless Driving ticket in Virginia, you can expect the attorney's legal fee to range anywhere from around $500 up to $2,500. I certainly do not charge anywhere near the high end of that range.

Generally speaking, public defenders have a bigger caseload and a higher volume of more serious cases that consume a lot of their time. Whereas private attorneys have a smaller caseload and a lower volume of more serious cases that consume a lot of their time. This means that a private attorney can devote more time into not only working your case, but also communicating with you before court to ensure a proper and optimal defense.

How Can I Help My Attorney Get The Best Result Of My Case?

You can help your attorney get the best result of your case by providing the right information and documents to your attorney before court. This includes providing and obtaining all of the information and documents on pages 55 – 58 and 92 – 93.

If you have any questions or concerns about your case, you may call or text me on my office phone at (757) 394-3434 or email me at mhuff@hufflawplc.com.

NOTES

Made in the USA
Middletown, DE
07 April 2021